HOW TO TAME YOUR CAT

Attach ornaments with string and they won't make such a satisfying "thunk" noise.

SAM HART

ILLUSTRATED BY TATIANA DAVIDOVA

summersdale

HOW TO TAME YOUR CAT

Copyright © Summersdale Publishers Ltd, 2023

All rights reserved.

Text by Jess Zahra

Illustrations by Tatiana Davidova

No part of this book may be reproduced by any means, nor transmitted, nor translated into a machine language, without the written permission of the publishers.

An Hachette UK Company
www.hachette.co.uk

Summersdale Publishers Ltd
Part of Octopus Publishing Group Limited
Carmelite House
50 Victoria Embankment
LONDON
EC4Y 0DZ
UK

www.summersdale.com

Printed and bound in China

ISBN: 978-1-80007-712-6

Substantial discounts on bulk quantities of Summersdale books are available to corporations, professional associations and other organizations. For details contact general enquiries: telephone: +44 (0) 1243 771107 or email: enquiries@summersdale.com.

INTRODUCTION

Any cat parent will testify that beneath that
fluffy façade lurks the mind of an evil genius.
Cats are selectively deaf and they always
have a second agenda. However majestic or
composed they may seem, the wild beast
within is never far from the surface.
Luckily, this no-nonsense survival guide is
here to help you navigate your cat's quirks,
anticipate their evil plans and tame their
inner scratch-monster. The tips inside
this book are sure to mollify your moggy
and make you an elite cat owner in no
time — or just simply help you accept that
there's no way you will ever train a cat.

The more money
you lavish upon
your cat, the
less interested
they become.
They will reject
such obvious bids
for affection,
so don't waste
your money.

Don't wait for your
cat to nuzzle you.
Make the first move
by nuzzling them.

KNOW THAT NO
MATTER WHAT
TREAT YOU
PROVIDE FOR
YOUR CAT, THEY
WILL ALWAYS
EXPECT BETTER.

GET TO YOUR WALLS
BEFORE YOUR CAT DOES
AND DECORATE WITH
DISTRESSED WALLPAPER
AND CHAOTIC ART. THIS
WAY THEIR WORK HAS
BEEN DONE FOR THEM, AND
NOW THEY CAN RELAX.

IF THEY SEE A DOG DOING SOMETHING, CATS WILL DO THE OPPOSITE. USE THIS TO YOUR ADVANTAGE.

Learn that, no matter
how hard you try,
your cat will always
have the upper hand.

DOES YOUR CAT

WREAK HAVOC

WHEN THEY'RE HOME
ALONE? TAKE THEM
OUT AND ABOUT
IN A BESPOKE

CAT BACKPACK

SO YOU NEED
NEVER BE APART.

Your cat is
not blocking
the view;
they *are*
the view.

No matter what trick you try to pull, your cat will never make your life easy if a trip to the vet is on the cards.

PREPARE FOR
AN ATTACK OF
THE MIDNIGHT
ZOOMIES BY
ENSURING ALL
WINDOWS ARE
TIGHTLY SHUT.

IF YOU'RE LOOKING
FOR UNBRIDLED
LOVE, FORGET IT.
YOUR CAT WOULD
RATHER BE NAPPING.

INSTALL A
SECURITY-GRADE
TOILET-PAPER
GUARD TO AVOID
UNSOLICITED
HOMEMADE
CONFETTI.

You've only just let them out of the door and they're back through the cat flap asking to be let out again — understand that your cat is training you, not the other way round.

RULE NUMBER 1
IN CAT TAMING:

THERE IS NO WAY
TO TAME YOUR CAT.

Deck out your
home with
plenty of feline
paraphernalia
to prove the
 extent of
your worship.

Attach ornaments
with string and
they won't make
such a satisfying
"thunk" noise.

PREVENT *THIS* FROM HAPPENING BY LEARNING THE PRECISE MOMENT YOUR CAT GOES FROM "CUTE AND CUDDLY" TO "ATTACK MONSTER".

YOU DON'T KNOW WHAT YOUR CAT HAS LICKED BEFORE THEY DRINK FROM YOUR KITCHEN TAP. INSTALL A CAT FOUNTAIN TO SAFEGUARD YOUR HYGIENE RATING.

PLAY HEAVY METAL MUSIC AS LOUD AS YOU CAN SO YOUR CAT DOESN'T FEEL THE NEED TO SUSTAIN THAT SCREAMING SOLO ALL BY THEMSELVES.

Accept that
being a cat parent
is not a choice,
but a lifestyle.

Look on the bright side;
your cat's morning
screech is the perfect
wake-up call and means
you never have to
set an alarm again.

THERE IS A
HIGHLY VARIABLE,
SECRET NUMBER OF

TUMMY RUBS

YOUR CAT WILL
ALLOW BEFORE YOU
BECOME A HUMAN
SCRATCH POST. ONLY
INTENSE RESEARCH
WILL ENABLE YOU TO
CRACK THE CODE.

If in doubt,
shake the
treat bag.

Ditch the laser pointer and invest in a disco ball to boost your cat's cardio and keep them entertained for hours. Meanwhile, you can treat yourself to some well-earned rest.

CATS HAVE NO
UNDERSTANDING
OF PERSONAL
SPACE AND NO
RESPECT FOR
BOUNDARIES.

YOUR CAT BRINGS
YOU THOSE UNWANTED
GIFTS BECAUSE THEY
WORRY YOU DON'T
EAT ENOUGH. STUFF
YOUR FACE TO PUT
THEIR MIND AT EASE.

YOUR CAT IS NOT
HOGGING THE BED.
YOU HAVE BEEN GIVEN
A FREE HOT-WATER
BOTTLE TO SPOON,
AND ONE THAT WON'T
GET COLD EITHER!

You're nobody
till you've been
ignored by a cat.

BE PREPARED FOR
YOUR CAT TO MAKE

A BEELINE

FOR THE ONE PERSON
WITH ALLERGIES.
IT'S LIKE THEY HAVE

A RADAR

OR SOMETHING.

You can never find a cat when you want to, but they will make sure to time their entrance just when you don't want them to.

YOUR CAT IS NOT
BEING DIFFICULT
WHEN THEY DECIDE
TO OBSTRUCT THE
THOROUGHFARES OF
YOUR HOUSE; THEY
ARE CREATING A
BESPOKE OBSTACLE
COURSE TO KEEP
YOU FIGHTING FIT!

You can rely on your cat to find the least convenient place to make their bed — and you can be sure it won't be the expensive fur-lined basket you bought.

IF YOU'RE TIRED OF
YOUR CAT GIVING
YOU ACUPUNCTURE,
PUT THEIR KNEADING
SKILLS TO GOOD USE
AND EMPLOY THEM
AS YOUR FURRY
LITTLE SOUS-CHEF.

If all else fails,
there's always catnip.

BUILD REINFORCED,

EXTRA-HIGH WALLS

FOR YOUR CAT LITTER
TRAY SO THAT WHEN
YOUR FELINE FRIEND
FEELS THE NEED TO
EMPTY THE CONTENTS
ONTO THE FLOOR,
THEY'LL BE DEEPLY

DISAPPOINTED.

Your cat isn't interested in you 99 per cent of the time, but you can guarantee that the minute you don't want their attention, you have it.

Whatever you're doing, it will always be less important than your cat. Sometimes you just need a reminder.

YOUR CAT KNOWS THAT FOOD TASTES BETTER WHEN IT COMES FROM YOUR PLATE. DISTRACT THEM WITH A DECOY SO YOU CAN ENJOY YOUR MEALS IN PEACE.

ON YOUR FEET, LOSE
YOUR SEAT! TO STOP
YOUR CAT STEALING YOUR
SPOT, DEPLOY A BOX TO
CREATE A DISTRACTION.
BOXES ARE PORTALS TO
UTOPIA AND MUST BE
GUARDED AT ALL COSTS.

MAKE YOUR CAT THEIR
VERY OWN YEAR-ROUND
CHRISTMAS TREE.
WHEN THE REAL ONE
ARRIVES IN DECEMBER,
IT WILL HAVE LOST
ITS NOVELTY.

No matter how
hard you try to
domesticate your cat,
their inner hunter
will always prevail.

PRIORITIZE A PEDICURE.

IF YOU'RE ALWAYS COOING OVER YOUR CAT'S LITTLE TOE BEANS, THEY MIGHT WONDER WHAT THE FUSS IS ABOUT AND INSPECT YOURS. GIVE THEM NO GROUNDS

FOR CRITICISM.

Cats need
to scratch.
Get yours
a scratching
post and your
furniture will
be saved!

Cats love the daily
discipline of being
taken for a walk.

OR YOU COULD
JUST ACCEPT
THAT CATS ARE
UNTRAINABLE.

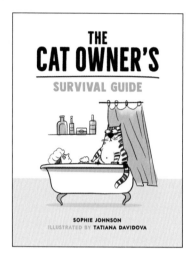

THE CAT OWNER'S SURVIVAL GUIDE

Sophie Johnson | Illustrated by Tatiana Davidova
978-1-80007-401-9 | Hardback

A hilarious, fully illustrated book of tongue-in-cheek advice for surviving life as a cat parent – the perfect gift for any cat lover. This book is here to teach you all the tricks you need to help you navigate life with your furry friend, so you can focus on the positives, like giving them head-scritches and cooing over their little toe beans.

THE DOG OWNER'S SURVIVAL GUIDE

Sophie Johnson | Illustrated by Tatiana Davidova
978-1-80007-400-2 | Hardback

A hilarious, fully illustrated book of tongue-in-cheek advice for surviving life as a dog parent – the perfect gift for any dog lover. Containing all the tricks you need to help you navigate life with your furry friend, so you can focus on the positives, like giving them head-scritches and nose-boops whenever they prove they're a good doggo.

Have you enjoyed this book?

If so, find us on Facebook at **Summersdale Publishers**, on Twitter at **@Summersdale** and on Instagram at **@summersdalebooks** and get in touch. We'd love to hear from you!

www.summersdale.com